KING CHARLES THE WISE

The Triumph of Universal Peace

A Masque

First published by O-Books, 2018
O-Books is an imprint of John Hunt Publishing Ltd., No. 3 East St., Alresford, Hampshire SO24 9EE, UK
office1@jhpbooks.net
www.johnhuntpublishing.com

For distributor details and how to order please visit the 'Ordering' section on our website.

Text copyright: Nicholas Hagger 2017

ISBN: 978 1 78535 847 0
978 1 78535 848 7 (ebook)
Library of Congress Control Number: 2017962532

A CIP catalogue record for this book is available from the British Library.

Design: Stuart Davies

Printed and bound by CPI Group (UK) Ltd, Croydon, CR0 4YY, UK

We operate a distinctive and ethical publishing philosophy in all areas of our business, from our global network of authors to production and worldwide distribution.

KING CHARLES THE WISE

The Triumph of Universal Peace

A Masque

Nicholas Hagger

BOOKS

Winchester, UK
Washington, USA

Also by Nicholas Hagger

Selected Stories: Follies and Vices of the Modern
Elizabethan Age
Selected Poems: Quest for the One
The Dream of Europa
Life Cycle and Other New Poems 2006 – 2016
The First Dazzling Chill of Winter
The Secret American Destiny
Peace for our Time
World State
World Constitution

"'Masque', a form of amateur histrionic entertainment, originally consisting of dancing and acting in dumb show, the performers being masked, afterwards including dialogue and song, 1562; a dramatic composition for this kind of entertainment, 1605."

The Shorter Oxford English Dictionary

"'Masque', a dramatic and musical entertainment, especially of the 16th and 17th centuries, originally of pantomime, later with metrical dialogue; a dramatic composition for this."

The Concise Oxford Dictionary

"Wisdom always discerns the direction
That pioneers a country's better way.
Folly claims to know the destination,
Its confidence leads citizens astray."

Nicholas Hagger, *King Charles the Wise*, p.41

"Let it be known, the Carolingian Age
Will seek to bring a universal peace
To humankind, regardless of nation."

Nicholas Hagger, *King Charles the Wise*, p.45

The front cover shows the Throne Room at Buckingham Palace with (left) Minerva, goddess of Wisdom, receiving Wisdom in rays from the Light (1896, mosaic artist Elihu Vedder, image in the Library of Congress prints and photography division, photograph explicitly placed in the public domain by Carol Highsmith in 2007); and (right) HRH Prince Charles, the Prince of Wales.

CONTENTS

Dramatis Personae

Characters in order of appearance:

Zeus
Minerva
His Royal Highness, Prince Charles, the Prince of Wales
Chorus of royal household staff
9 Shades of Kings and leaders
  Alfred
  Harold II
  William I, Conqueror
  Henry II
  Henry VIII
  George III
  Lord Palmerston
  Winston Churchill
  Keir Hardie
Britannia, goddess of the UK
Chorus of British people
Europa, goddess of Europe
Columbia, goddess of the US
Astraea, goddess of fairness
Penia, goddess of poverty
Pheme, goddess of rumour
Chorus of UN dignitaries
Chorus of suffering peoples
Apollo, god of Light and the sun
Chorus of 8 distinguished supporters
  Truman
  Eisenhower
  Einstein
  Churchill
  Russell
  Gandhi

J.F. Kennedy
Gorbachev
Clio, Muse of history
Chorus of historical leaders from British Empire and Commonwealth
Chorus of the world's united peoples
Chorus of 9 Muses
Chorus of 5 world leaders
Trump
Putin
Xi-Jinping
Juncker
Singh

Locations:

Mount Olympus
The Throne Room, Buckingham Palace, London

Preface
A Court Masque and Universal Peace

Early English court masques
The 16th- and early-17th-century masques in Europe and England were court entertainments. They celebrated an event at court, sometimes a royal marriage, and flattered the monarch.

In the early English masques Henry VIII, James I and Charles I all had masked non-speaking parts. In England Ben Jonson's early-17th-century masques were performed in the Banqueting Hall of the Whitehall Palace during Christmas, often on Twelfth Night. The Banqueting Hall was replaced by the Banqueting House, which was built between 1619 and 1622. Masques can be found in the works of Shakespeare (*A Midsummer Night's Dream*, *Henry VIII*, *The Tempest*), Milton (*Comus*), Shelley (*The Masque of Anarchy*) and most recently William Empson (*The Birth of Steel*). Empson's masque was in honour of the Queen's visit to Sheffield in 1954 and addressed Queen Elizabeth II as a "goddess". (The Queen returned the compliment by knighting Empson in 1979.)

Origins of the masque
The masque seems to have originated in "mumming", a masked mime which Richard II took part in as early as 1377. The Italian masquerade was a carnival entertainment, and in France there were masked performances. Throughout Europe there were "guisings" or "disguisings" in which an allegorical figure addressed a courtly audience. Dumbshows can be found in Kyd's *The Spanish Tragedy* (first performed 1587) and Shakespeare's *A Midsummer Night's Dream* (1595–1596, the wedding of Pyramus and Thisbe), *Hamlet* (1500–1602) and *Pericles, Prince of Tyre* (1607–1608). Masques performed before Elizabeth I (including an anti-Catholic masque performed before her at the Whitehall Palace on Twelfth Night, 6 January 1559) emphasised the unity of her kingdom and the peace and concord that flourished in her realm.

Masque's five sections

The masque had five sections: the prologue; the antimasque (a spectacle of disorder and chaos); the masque (which transformed the disorder into order and harmony, and provided a resolution); the revels (which rejoiced at the resolution); and the epilogue.

The Dream of Europa: The Triumph of Peace

My first masque, *The Dream of Europa* (2015), celebrated the 70 years of European peace that followed the Second World War. It was in five sections and was subtitled *The Triumph of Peace*.

King Charles the Wise: The Triumph of Universal Peace

This masque, *King Charles the Wise*, is about the UK's global role after the disorder of Brexit and the birth of a united and unified world. In the prologue Zeus asks Minerva (the goddess of Wisdom) to work for world peace by promoting a democratic, federal World State strong enough to abolish war. He sees the founding of such a World State as the UK's new global role and asks her to establish whether the UK's Prince of Wales can be persuaded to support the concept when talking to world leaders. In the antimasque world citizens chant their misery and wretchedness at the disorder and chaos in the world, and the goddesses Britannia, Europa and Columbia (speaking for the UK, the EU and the US respectively) give their own discordant perspectives on the UK's future role. In the masque Minerva turns the disorder into order and provides a resolution: a coming World State that will unify humankind and bring the prospect of universal peace. Prince Charles approves the humanitarian principles and concerns on which this new age of peace will be based, and she crowns him with her Wisdom. In the revels, historical figures and contemporary world citizens rejoice at the prospect of a unified world. In the epilogue Minerva reports back to Zeus, who will now send her to the Secretary-General of the UN.

This masque contrasts the contemporary disorder with the order of a coming democratic World State which will be strong enough to abolish war. It calls for a unified world with a limited supranational World Government that can solve humankind's problems. Its call comes at a time when in every continent there are divided nation-states and problems – such as wars, terrorist attacks, refugees and the threat of nuclear extermination – that seem insoluble within the present world structures.

Although the coming coronation of the Prince of Wales is referred to, the court event this masque celebrates is the UK's role in delivering a new structure that can bring universal peace. It presents humankind's need to bring the world together beyond the separateness of populism and isolationism. Political Universalism, a form of global governance in which all humankind can have a say, is on the world's coming political agenda and aims to establish universal peace. And so *King Charles the Wise* is subtitled *The Triumph of Universal Peace*.

Dialectic between opposites
In all my works there is a dialectic in which two opposites are reconciled in a unity in accordance with the algebraic formula I found in the East, $+A + -A = 0$. My two masques conform to a dialectic involving disorder and order. *The Dream of Europa* celebrated the peace-bringing EU, and this masque, *King Charles the Wise*, celebrates the UK's new global role that can bring in universal peace. These two masques are themselves opposites that suggest $+A$ and $-A$, the first being on Europe and the second on the UK's Brexit, both of which are reconciled within the World State. Similarly, this masque about the UK's post-Brexit future, *King Charles the Wise*, will be contradicted by its opposite, a mock-heroic long poem in progress about the circumstances surrounding the UK's departure from the European Union, 'Fools' Paradise', and both are similarly reconciled within the World State.

Performance and production
A word on performance. A production could be performed by a cast of six (Zeus, Minerva, Prince Charles and the three royal household staff) with all the other characters – the five goddesses, the nine Kings and leaders and various choruses – shown on screen. Indeed, the Prologue and Epilogue could be shown on screen to indicate the remoteness of the gods' Olympus, and so Zeus could be pre-recorded on screen, leaving a cast of five on stage. However, if all the other characters are

pre-recorded on screen the interaction between Prince Charles and the goddesses on stage would be lost, as would the on-stage audience for Minerva's crowning. The principle is that the left screen is the link between Buckingham Palace and Olympus (Zeus and the goddesses)/ the future, and the right screen is the link between Buckingham Palace and choruses (from the past, present and future, alive or dead, including the nine Kings and leaders and the shades of the dead). Such an approach would cut performance costs.

Genesis of this masque

I have had this masque in mind for some time. In a letter to the Prince of Wales on 1 August 2016 I wrote:

I see your coming reign as being distinctive, as I predicted in 'Night Visions in Charlestown' in 1983 (p.499 in *Collected Poems* with notes on pp.554–556). It can bring new hope for humankind by pioneering a new solution to the world's problems: a new spiritual vision of the unity of all humankind that can advance the lives of all people everywhere. As King you can be perceived as standing for universal values – Defender of the Faiths and more – and can come to be seen as King Charles the Wise. I do seriously intend to put this vision into a masque when I get clear of my immediate duties.

I had been thinking deeply about the UK's future global role after Brexit and the UK's possible hand in a coming World State, but first I had to write *Peace for our Time* and then *World State* and *World Constitution* (all 2018).

Although it may seem that my Muse put my poetic inspiration in touch with Zeus and Minerva as I sipped at the Pierian spring in the shadow of Mount Olympus, this masque presents the UK's innovative shaping of a new world structure that can bring in an era of universal peace and prosperity and benefit the whole of humankind.

21 August; 22 September; 16, 18 October; 16 November 2017

The Genius of Literature presenting her pupils to Minerva
Stipple engraving, print by John Chapman, 1793; after Daniel Dodd,
published by J. Wilkes

Minerva, goddess of Wisdom, greeting two pupils with linked arms;
the Genius of Literature as an angel on a cloud taking the man's hand
and pointing towards a 'sun' (the Light) inscribed 'Literature' and
emblazoned with implements for study (a harp, a globe, a palette)
and cherub heads

KING CHARLES THE WISE

Prologue

(Early August 2017, Mount Olympus. ZEUS is seated on the Olympian throne, spotlit. He is wise, shrewd and sophisticated-looking, but he is slightly doddery and no longer all powerful, and running the world is difficult. He is doing his best. The gods cannot control what humans do but they can try to influence events after humans have exercised their free will in a chaotic way. He addresses all the gods and goddesses. There are two screens on the stage, one on the left and one on the right.)

Zeus: What's wrong with humankind? I want a world
Without war, famine and disease, that's like
A harvest paradise where souls ripen
Like apples on an orchard's apple trees
In tranquil sunshine on a summer's day,
Where bees nuzzle in fragrant lavender
And dandelions smile under fluffy clocks
And swans glide beside fields of golden corn.
But men fight each other, leaders squabble.
It's hopeless, humankind is in a mess
And we gods and goddesses have to save
Recalcitrant humans from their mistakes.
We have to intervene discreetly when
We can, when there's an opportunity,
To influence individuals who'll accept
Our policies and adopt what we want.
Europe's in turmoil, again. The UK
Has left without a plan, there is a hole
In the EU's budget. And yet again
Political leaders have let us down
By thinking nation-state and not seeing
The wider unity we all desire.

We need stability so the EU
Can expand to a *bloc* of fifty states
And the half-blind UK leaders can grasp
Their country's true destiny, its role in
Bringing to birth a world that's free from war.
I preside over all created forms,
All species of wildlife and humankind,
And in my grander scheme of things Brexit
Is only important as it allows
The UK to bring in our new order.
I can see the UK's new destiny
To change the world's structure after Brexit
So clearly, yet all British citizens
Seem unaware of what's ahead for them.
An independent UK'll be well placed
To move between the US and Europe,
China, Russia, India and all countries.
The UK is very innovative
And's always been very influential.
The UK's one of the five Permanent
Members of the Security Council.
It's one of the five most respected states,
It's had the fifth-largest economy
And the fifth-largest military as well.
The UK's the right country to bring peace,
It is the only Permanent Member
Of the Security Council that can.
The UK's ruling class do not see this,
They lack urgency as if in a dream.
Its leader's on a three-week walking tour.
She's like a shy doe on a mountainside,
And she's as slow as a plodding tortoise.
She thinks the UK can break free from all
European laws while continuing
To benefit from the single market.
Her policy is foolish, I despair.

Following her disastrous election
She is politically unstable.
Her party's divided, the extreme Right
Has captured the centre, she's a puppet
Amid the self-interested agendas
Of ambitious and treacherous back-stabbers
Who prowl like hungry wolves eyeing their prey.
Both parties are controlled from their extremes,
Voters honk like geese hearing intruders.
Fourteen months have slipped by since the Leave vote
And negotiations have not progressed.
What's done cannot be undone, the UK
Is going to separate, and its PM
May not be in power next year. A vote
Of no confidence or a letter signed
By forty-eight MPs may see her off.
I need to look beyond this current bout
Of UK disorder and confusion,
Incompetence, arrogant self-interest.
The politicians are all transient
And have closed minds as they are partisan.
The one enduring thing's the monarchy.
But the Queen is now in her twilit years.
The key person to focus on behind
The Government's her heir and successor,
The Prince of Wales. He will endure, we can
Regard him as a 'permanent' monarch.
And he's proved to be more open-minded
Than partisan politicians who toe
Their party line and will not think outside
Their box of narrow party loyalty.
He is respected and is the best placed
To give our vision global prominence.
His world-view's sound. He's attuned to the world –
The environment and the countryside,
Conservation, architecture, global

Warming, sustainability, the young,
Regeneration of communities –
And it's clear to the world that he has soul.
He believes in the divine right of kings.
I'm sure he'll listen to our policies
With an open, humanitarian mind.
He must now be the best prepared monarch
Ever, he's trained for over sixty years.
It's a hereditary monarchy,
He cannot be bypassed for his own heir.
There's no one else who could speak out for world
Unity: President Trump is useless
With his America-First policy;
Both the Russian and Chinese leaderships
Are focused on their own regional *blocs*;
The EU President has to expand
The EU and that will take all his time.
Only the UK can bring about change
And call for the UN to be transformed
Into a new World State as is our plan.
There may be some initial disquiet
That power will shift from the West to the East,
But that's already happening and new
Constituencies in every region
Will prevent this and ensure that the West
Has a role in shaping the coming world.
An elected World State's the only way.
It's the future, it has to be. And we
Are all agreed, it's a UK project.
I know there is disunity within
My 'Cabinet' and several of you have
Different views as to how the Prince should rule,
But now's the time to thrash differences out
So there's a one-'Cabinet' view that will
Include the long-term perspective we want
That will bring peace and unity for all.

I know he'll be a constitutional
Monarch and will have to tread carefully,
But it's time for the Prince to be aware
Of the gods' vision of the world's future.
And so I have decided to send down
Not Hermes but our goddess of Wisdom.
My dear Minerva – you were Athena
To the Greeks but Minerva to great Rome
And I still think of you as Minerva –
I want you to be my ambassador
As a robin befriends a gardener.
Descend to him and discuss the UK's
Destiny under his reign, and lead him
Forward into wisdom as only you
Know how to, and then report back to me.

Minerva: I'm honoured to be asked to undertake
Such an important mission. We all know
That to unite the world the fifty states
Of the US and (under Europa's
Clear guidance) Europe's future fifty states
Must combine with the Far East's fifty states
(Sadly not yet assembled), and we know
That the UK may quite soon be the best-
Placed to lead this united world forward.
And we know it could propose a World State
Before the new states join regional *blocs*.
I agree the US, Russia, China
And the EU can't be depended on
To change the world, and that this role best suits
The UK. Its politicians are all
Hopeless, I agree that it needs a man
With higher consciousness who knows the One
And the vision of unity, and Charles,
Though soon a constitutional monarch,
Has already shown this by declaring

That he will defend *all* faiths, not *the* faith
Of Christendom alone. All can now see
He has a Universalist outlook
And therefore is already wise. It's right
To work with him to support his wisdom.
Lord of all, I am now ready to start.

Zeus: Excellent, dear Minerva. But there must
First be a thrash-out of conflicting views.
Britannia, Europa, Columbia
And others among the gods' 'Cabinet'
Who wish to persuade him of their own way,
Those of us gods who speak for the choices
Of destiny the UK must still make
(In exercise of its free will, for all
Countries have free choices that we respect
But influence by our diplomacy)
Will take part in a free-for-all debate
So, democratic as ever, we all
Are of one mind and share a consensus
As all Cabinets are supposed to do.
We will have one position, him and us,
So he can act for us. Oh, look, look here.

(PRINCE CHARLES, *sitting on the throne in the
Throne Room in Buckingham Palace, is visible on the left
screen. The throne is above three red-carpeted steps. He
is lit by a spotlight from electrical equipment left behind,
together with two screens and a laptop, by a technical
crew. The chandelier before the throne is too high to be
seen and is anyway unlit. He is sitting on the red-and-
gold throne, one of two identical grand chairs. His red
box is on the other chair, open, and he is holding sheets
of paper. With his free hand from time to time he drums
his fingers on the lid of the red box. To his right is an
all-in-one tea tray with handles and legs.)*

I've got him on my screen. See, he's alone
In the Throne Room in Buckingham Palace,
Sitting on the red-and-gold throne, bending,
Working on the Queen's red box, helping her
Deal with her State papers like a Regent,
Tapping like a woodpecker seeking grubs.
'Operation Hand-over' has started
In deed though the Queen denies it in name.
No one else is about, it's late evening.
You could catch him alone, if you are quick.

Minerva:

I'll go at once, knowing you'll be viewing
All that I do and hearing what I say.

(CHORUS OF ROYAL HOUSEHOLD STAFF. *Three of Buckingham Palace's 800 staff are behind a door off the Throne Room that is not properly closed: a footman, a page and a maid. They are on the edge of the stage to one side, between the action and the audience. They are waiting for Prince Charles to complete his work so they can do their routine chores and finish for the day. They are tired after a long day's work and whisper loudly to each other.*)

Chorus of
royal house-
hold staff:

Something is happening, we don't know what.
Something to do with Prince Charles, who we serve.
He left the Office of the Prince of Wales,
He's shut himself in the Throne Room to work
On papers in Her Majesty's red box.
He came from Clarence House this afternoon,
Worked in the Office of the Prince of Wales
And went through papers in the Queen's red box.
He was called to the Throne Room as there was
A talk and presentation with two screens

For the Family and senior staff,
A confidential kind of conference
Before the throne in the late afternoon.
The electrical equipment and screens
Are still here, they'll be removed tomorrow.
At the end he returned to his Office
To sign letters for his secretaries
And finish his work on the Queen's red box.
He chose not to go back to Clarence House
But then decided he would come back here
To the Throne Room – to ponder what he'd seen
On the screens, while doing his paperwork?

(*The* THREE CHORUS MEMBERS *speak the next three lines individually.*)

I, the page, carried in his red box. I,
The footman, clicked the spotlight. I, the maid,
Brought a tea tray and something light to eat.
He's not to be disturbed, we can't go in.
We think he's pondering the commercial
Viability of opening the State
Rooms, new parts of this Palace and the grounds
To the public full-time when the Queen's gone
As he won't be moving from Clarence House.
We think that's what the conference was about,
That the screens showed where the public can go.
Where will that leave us? Will we still have jobs?
He's alone in this atmospheric place
And poring over papers in his box.
We don't know how long he will be in there.
We've had a long day, it will soon be time
To finish up and go off to our rooms.
So we are waiting until we're summoned.
It wasn't always like this in the past
Before the Queen grew old and had to share

Her work. Those were good days, we were on call.
Alas, those times have passed and won't return.

Page:

I am waiting to carry his red box
Back to the Office of the Prince of Wales.

Maid:

I'll clear away the tea tray when he leaves.

Footman:

I'll click off the spotlight when he retires.

Antimasque

Prince Charles: I'm back again at Monarchy HQ.
The Queen has taken a step back along
With my father, the Duke of Edinburgh,
And I am taking up the slack they've left.
I shall lay the Queen's wreath on Remembrance
Sunday at the Cenotaph. My time's come.
'Operation Hand-over' has begun.
I'd rather be in cosy Clarence House
Than rattle here in Buckingham Palace.
I've done this for a while, but this is bad.
I've read these State papers but I am none
The wiser regarding the Government's
EU position, which is like a stag
In thick undergrowth. It seems we'll leave both
The single market and customs union
But after a short transition period.
I read two options, delayed for two years.
I think May may not know what to do next.
I think she's buying time to think it through,
I think she's at bay like a fox from hounds.
Delaying 'out' till the next election
Will keep the economy strong till then
And see her party through to a poll win.
I think she has been playing for safety,

13

And keeping her split Cabinet at one.
But the thought in my mind, which I can't seem
To remove, is: I really want to know
Where the UK is going when it leaves
The EU. That is not in these papers.
We're on a bridge, what's our destination?
Everything is disorderly, I find
It all bewildering. I can't get rid
Of that nagging thought: where are we going?

(MINERVA *materialises beside him from the shadows and stands before the spotlight.*)

Minerva: That's because I put that thought in your mind.

Prince Charles: Who are you? How did you get in? How did
                  You get past the Palace security?

Minerva: I am Minerva, I've been in your thoughts
                  Because I can confer wisdom on Kings.

Prince Charles: Minerva, you are goddess of Wisdom.

(*He stares at her and rubs his eyes and shakes his head.*)

Some ask what sort of a King I will be.
Will I send meddling letters to the State's
Ministers, will they be words of wisdom?
I wish I had the wisdom of a sage
Who's thought deeply and absorbed the wisdom
Of the East and the West, abstruse knowledge
Philosophers have unearthed in themselves
Like nuggets of gold they clean and polish.
Then I could read this turgid stuff and know
At once with clarity what it all means
And what destination it's advising,

Get to the essence of what's being said
Like spotting a newt in a murky pond.

(PRINCE CHARLES *sighs*.)

Minerva: You *have* thought deeply, I can tell. You are
                  Original, work things out for yourself.
                  You're no stranger to wisdom, you have said
                  Some challenging things that are very wise.

Prince Charles: 'What is wisdom?' I ask myself. Perhaps
                  I have it already to some degree
                  Or like to think I have it, and perhaps
                  It's come out in what I have had to say
                  On 'my topics', such as the environment.
                  You were shown as an owl on ancient coins.
                  Perhaps I too am a bit of an owl.

Minerva: I have come as Zeus's ambassador.
                  The gods are very interested in you
                  And what you may achieve when you are King,
                  What direction you'll take the UK in.
                  Admit you've thought of Minerva –

Prince Charles: I have –

Minerva: And now you've conjured me and now I'm here.
                  How do you see the UK's destiny?

Prince Charles: It's bewildering. In twenty years' time....
                  There have been promises but there's no plan.
                  I don't know what a hard Brexit involves.
                  I can see several UK destinies
                  And several directions. Not all are good.

Minerva: I'm not alone, the nine Muses conjured

15

These nine shades from your glorious history
Who all have views on what should happen next:

(NINE SHADES *are now in the dimly-lit Throne Room
and stand before the spotlight when they are mentioned.*)

The Kings Alfred and Harold the Second,
William Conqueror, Henry the Second,
Henry the Eighth and George the Third; also
Politicians Palmerston and Churchill.
And Keir Hardie who speaks for all the poor.
They greet you from the underworld, six are
Your ancestors and want you to do right.
They sympathise with your predicament
And feel protective as you make your choice.
Each one has advice on your destiny.
Note I say 'your' and not just 'the UK's',
For what you choose will shape your country's course
As you make Brexit work with new thinking,
But will also define *your* destiny.
And other goddesses are in this room.
Sit back and listen, and judge what they say.
At the end I'll ask for your opinion.
First here's Britannia, who was shown with shield
On the old, pre-European penny.

(BRITANNIA, *carrying a shield and trident and wearing
a Corinthian helmet, stands before the spotlight.*)

Britannia: Your Royal Highness, your first love's Britain.
                    Listen to the British people's comments.

(*A* CHORUS OF BRITISH PEOPLE, *a cross-section
of all classes and professions, some in suits and some
casually dressed, comes up on the right screen.*)

Chorus of British people:	We, the British people, are miserable. State workers have had no rise for eight years. It's all cuts and repaying deficit. We are resentful, so we voted Leave And to slash the Tories' majority. We have messed up what they wanted. That's good. We dream of prosperity but despair. Life's hard, it's hard to make ends meet, but some Live in luxury and we're envious. Our tower blocks are not safe and no one cares. Our anger may explode in violent rage. We old folk have stolen our children's dreams. We all disparage our hopeless leaders. Who will lead us into prosperity?

(BRITANNIA *addresses* PRINCE CHARLES.)

Britannia:	You will be King of the UK and will Address the grievances you have just heard, All consequences of the EU's rules. Its bureaucracy and hard-line bankers Have led to Europe-wide austerity That stirred the UK's revolt and Brexit. The EU fog's shrouded Britain's glory. The UK is being liberated, It's heading for independence. Always Remember, UK First, Little England, Control immigrants, no EU freedom Of movement, but soft border with Ireland. Be isolationist, do not take part In foreign adventures off North Korea. Scotland, Wales and Northern Ireland all have Devolved parliaments, but England does not. Look after England, nurture the English Nation-state as the bedrock of your throne.

Mark my words, as a spider, its web spun,
Waits for flies May will soon go to Florence
And make a speech that's conciliatory
And requests an 'implementing' period
Of two years, during which the UK'll make
Full payments into the EU's budget.
The EU will make concessions, it wants
A deal for its car manufacturers.
There can be a deal: as a blue tit pecks
On a bird feeder yet is free to fly
So the UK can have full benefits
From the single market's supply of goods
And control over freedom of movement.
Don't forget, most of the EU nations
Were occupied by Hitler and were saved
By the UK, which liberated France
And so many other countries. It's time
For them to show their gratitude and make
Concessions so there can be a good deal.
It's now the pay-back time for the EU.
But if there is 'no deal', then no matter.
Britain will survive and be great again.
Nothing's agreed till everything's agreed.
'No deal' may be best, the UK'll pay less.
Without 'no deal' the payments will be huge.
The UK wouldn't agree a figure
But a method of calculating one.
When a trade deal with the EU's agreed
The UK would agree to pay for all
Its liabilities and commitments,
Its share of the current EU budget,
Long-term projects, loans and pensions accrued
Over forty-four years of membership,
Inaccurately called an 'exit fee':
Seventy-eight billion pounds gross, net (after
The UK's share of the EU's assets

Has been taken into account) at least
Thirty-five billion pounds after leaving,
Could rise to thirty-nine billion as it's
Not known how long the pensioners will live.
The true cost would not be known for decades.
But there's also the thirty billion pounds
The UK'll pay from the referendum
To the date of leaving. The full total
Is therefore nearly *seventy* billion pounds,
Cheaper than the *five hundred* billion pounds
For remaining in for forty-two years.
(That's twelve billion a year times forty-two.)
But even so it's far too high a price.
Is a 'good trade deal' over forty years
Worth seventy billion pounds? I don't think so.
'No deal' would save us from this vast outlay.
And remember why Brexit's a good thing:
No annual payments of twelve billion pounds,
New control over immigrants and laws
And escape from the hopeless MEPs
And the undemocratic Commission
That's like a heron watching our *koi* carp.
It's better than being a vassal state
Of the EU in perpetuity.
Either way, deal or no deal, you are best
To put the UK first, and follow me.

(ALFRED THE GREAT, HAROLD II *and* HENRY
VIII *stand before the spotlight in turn.*)

Alfred the Great: Unite the UK from the EU's Danes.

Harold II: Repel invasions from Norman Europe.

Henry VIII: Stand up to Europe with its Papal seat
That's always opposed Protestantism.

Prince Charles: I am of European descent, I
Have German, Greek and Danish blood, but I
Have sympathy with some of what you say,
Though I have the world in my soul. I'm not
Isolationist, I'm rather global.

Britannia: But also from your island, rule the waves
And spread UK influence round the globe.
In your mind and the minds of your subjects
I am still seated on a rock with shield
And trident, clad in Corinthian helmet.
England can be alone yet span the seas.

(PALMERSTON *and* CHURCHILL *stand before the spotlight in turn.*)

Palmerston: You need to rebuild the British Empire
That ruled the waves in the Victorian Age –

Churchill: And ruled a quarter of the world before
The First World War weakened its mighty sway
And the Second World War bankrupted it.

Prince Charles: History has moved on, there's no going back.
The imperial time was great, but it's now gone.
The dominions cannot be as they were.
Martial Britannia, you stand for conquest.
The UK's destiny is not empire –
Not empire restored, not a new empire.
Some other destiny is the UK's.

(CHORUS OF ROYAL HOUSEHOLD STAFF, *loud whispering.*)

Chorus of royal house- hold staff:	He's got a visitor. We don't know who. This place is far too large to be a home. There are seven hundred and seventy-five rooms And many corridors and entrance doors. We now think he's rehearsing for a film. He's got some actors who're speaking with him. They must have arrived from the Quadrangle And been escorted up the Grand Staircase And made their way through the Green Drawing Room. We don't think he's promoting this Palace Commercially, not now. We think that was Happening at the conference this afternoon. He's talking about Brexit. We hear bits, And some of what we hear is worrying. Brexit has not gone well. The UK's role Is in chaos. Many are miserable. We are alarmed at what Brexit might bring. The actress playing Britannia has made A stirring speech on the English. Will he Make Britain great again when he succeeds Her Majesty? Will he revive our dream, The British Dream of endless betterment So children do better than their parents? What kind of King will he be, and how strong?
Minerva:	And here's Europa, goddess of Europe.
	(EUROPA, *Cretan moon goddess and goddess of Europe, stands before the spotlight. She addresses* PRINCE CHARLES *and copes with* BRITANNIA's *interruptions by answering them and then returns her attention to* PRINCE CHARLES.)
Europa:	Your Royal Highness, you are Europe's friend.

21

The EU's expanding to fifty states.
Six Western Balkan countries will soon join:
Macedonia, Montenegro, Serbia,
Albania, Kosovo, and Bosnia and
Herzegovina. The EU's growing
Into a United States of Europe.
The UK is going against the trend,
It's like a branch being lopped from the tree
Of European civilization.
You must urge your Government to stay in
The single market as it now exports
Forty-four per cent of the goods you trade
(Worth two hundred and twenty-four billion
Pounds a year) to the EU. If it walks
Away from this like a mouse vacating
A well-stocked larder having sniffed some cheese
In a mousetrap, it won't make up the gap
By trading with the non-EU countries.
The EU's a noble undertaking,
Created to prevent war by locking
Countries into institutions for trade,
A tribute to Adenauer and de Gaulle
Who, though once enemies, signed a Treaty
Of Friendship: European integration
That has brought peace to Brussels-ruled Europe
For seventy years when for a thousand years
Before that there were European wars
Every generation, most recently
Two world wars. You must urge your Government
To reverse Brexit, stay in the EU.
In a new referendum the public
Will vote to Remain now that they have seen
The worsening that voting Leave will mean.

Britannia: Excuse me for interrupting, but you
Are wrong, the public would again vote Leave

Like magpies chasing off a sparrowhawk.
There is no worsening, and quite simply
A second referendum won't happen.

Europa: It *can* happen. You have to understand
That most involved are heading for 'no deal'.
The EU want 'no deal' to make it clear
That exiting the EU brings bad terms
That won't be copied by the twenty-seven.
They'll hope Britain will tire and end Brexit.
The Brexiteers want 'no deal' so they can
Get the UK out of the EU now
And dodge the thirty-five-billion-pound fee
Like a squirrel that's guarding buried nuts.
The Remain MPs would like a 'no deal'
As delay may unsettle the public,
Who may have second thoughts about Brexit
And so call to Remain in the EU.
May could progress to a deal if she pays
The thirty-five-billion-pound exit fee
But fears the Brexiteers and DUP
Will oppose in the Commons and bring on
An election at which she'll be thrown out.
She's offered just twenty billion euros.
She'll head for 'no deal', and a soft border.
So all sides will advance to a 'no deal'
On Christmas Day, the EU's deadline day.
But 'no deal' can result in a second
Referendum. Like a fox stalking hens
Near a hen-coop May will visit Florence
But the EU will not make concessions.
The UK can go slow on the divorce –
On rights of EU citizens, Irish
Borders, how many billions will be sent
To honour commitments – and so provoke
A breakdown in the talks, and can then call

23

A second referendum to confirm
That all are happy with 'no deal', and with
Economic slow-down, no cheap-flight slots,
Worse still, no flights to or from the EU,
Hospital closures, banking exodus,
Increasing deficits, sinking standards.
The EU'll want Northern Ireland to split
From the UK so the Irish border
With the UK will be the Irish Sea.
Alarmed, the people *can* vote 'Remain'. Or
(A different scenario, but same outcome)
If there's a deal UK MPs must choose
To accept it or else reject Brexit,
To take the deal or leave it and remain.
The EU can make the agreement so
Unpalatable to UK MPs –
'Our final offer, or call off Brexit' –
That next summer the British Parliament
Recoils in horror and votes Brexit down.
May can then revoke Article 50
And apply to rejoin by invoking
Article 49, on getting in –
And win at the next general election.
Your Royal Highness, Remain can still win.
'No deal''s the way back into the EU.

Britannia: You know the Crown is above politics.
The public won't vote Remain, nor MPs.
Exorbitant demands have slowed progress.
The UK won't pay a huge exit fee.
It's blackmail, and we simply will not pay.
We can manage on our own, and we can't
Afford the thirty-five billion you want.
The date we leave will be enshrined in law.
If our MPs don't like the final deal
We'll leave without a deal on the due date.

Europa: And what if both sides want to keep the talks
                     Going beyond that date to settle things?
                     You're in bad shape, you can't stand on your own.
                     It's going to be announced that you've lost
                     Half a trillion pounds that has gone missing,
                     The UK's net international assets
                     Have collapsed after being revalued,
                     The UK is 490[1]
                     Billion pounds poorer than was thought. Instead
                     Of a surplus of 469[2] billion
                     There's a net deficit of twenty-two
                     Billion, and the UK no longer has
                     A reserve of net foreign assets that
                     Can protect its economy if it
                     Has to defend sterling and debt markets.
                     The UK needs the EU right now as
                     A lolloping rabbit needs its burrow.

Britannia: No, foreign assets owned by companies,
                     Banks and individuals are investments made
                     Overseas. They are estimated by
                     The National Statistics Office, which makes
                     An estimate based on a formula,
                     Which it has just revised, 'losing' billions.
                     Change the formula and the amount's changed.
                     The UK *can* still stand on its own feet,
                     And like a pheasant in a country lane
                     Bring joy to all who see its unspoilt life.

                     (EUROPA *sighs and ignores* BRITANNIA.)

Europa: Your Royal Highness, go 'no deal' and stay.
                     The EU will welcome the UK back
                     Like a sheep that strayed from one of its farms.
                     Of course, the Major opt-out will have gone
                     And the Thatcher rebate, and the pound will

Go when the UK joins the eurozone
And becomes part of the United States
Of Europe that will have its own army
And stand up to Russia on its borders,
But you will enjoy great prosperity.
'No Brexit' is better than a good deal,
And is much better than a sour 'no deal'.
Your Royal Highness, it's a no-brainer.

(WILLIAM THE CONQUEROR *and* HENRY II *stand before the spotlight in turn. They address* PRINCE CHARLES.)

William the
Conqueror: Allow the EU to take full control
Of all decisions, for soon the UK
Will benefit as the EU expands
Into a United States of Europe.

Henry II: Remember when England ruled part of France
Within the Angevin Empire, remain
In the EU if you possibly can.

Prince Charles: I sympathise with much of what you say.
I am a European, I belong
To the European civilization.
We British share European history:
The Catholic, then the Protestant rulers.
But as I will be King of the UK
And Brexit means leaving once and for all
I am deeply aware that the UK
Has its own destiny. It's been the fifth-
Largest economy in the world, it's
A major power in its own right and should
Be governed from the UK, not Brussels.
I'm pro-European but the UK

Must chart a different course that's its own course.

(MINERVA *nods*. CHORUS OF ROYAL HOUSEHOLD STAFF, *loud whispering*.)

Chorus of
royal house-
hold staff: Did you hear that? It's all about Europe.
The EU lady was pressing him hard.
Poor Charles, he's supposed to be doing his work
And they're distracting him, he can't get on.
It doesn't seem to be a rehearsal.
It seems to be for real, but who are they?

Minerva: Columbia speaks for America.

(COLUMBIA, *the Lady Liberty of the Statue of Liberty who sometimes takes the form of an Indian queen, is spotlit. She speaks with an American accent.*)

Columbia: Your Royal Highness, you *love* the US.
The US and the UK've always had
A special relationship. Some will say
This only worked at the end of the War;
That only Israel's special to us now
Because it has influence in Congress;
That Obama scoffed at the UK as
Its PMs were poodles during the wars;
That Trump's 'America-First' will be tough.
But our relationship goes much deeper
Than these shallow perceptions. We both speak
English as our main language. We are tied
Together by history and our values
As military allies in two world wars.
Our financial systems are in accord,
Our interconnecting computer wires

Tangle like brambles in a blackberry hedge.
The UK's an island, it stands apart
From the European utopia.
From once ruling a quarter of the world
The UK's in decline. From the foremost
Post-war economic power in Europe
It's slid to an offshore island that's ceased
To matter, its view no longer matters.
It's an isolated old people's home
That can't pay for itself. It's insular.
So apply to be the fifty-first state
Of the USA. That is the UK's
Destiny, to join the United States.

Britannia: You're forgetting a deal with the EU.

(COLUMBIA *copes with* BRITANNIA's *interruption
and then continues to address* PRINCE CHARLES.)

Columbia: Forget what's happening with the EU,
Or rather, what's not happening, for the talks
Will be deadlocked. The UK will not pay
A penny till they know there's a trade deal,
And the EU will want what's budgeted
Before they discuss any future deal,
They'll press for this in writing urgently.
May will attempt to breach the deadlock by
Travelling to Brussels. At leaders' level,
A suppliant at the evening banquet
At the European Council's summit
Like a peacock displaying its false eyes
She'll plead that trade talks should begin at once.
They'll say too little progress has been made,
But perhaps at their December meeting –
If she will pay a whopping exit fee.
But time's now too short for a bespoke deal,

Only an off-the-shelf deal's on offer,
Like the deal Norway has, which May's against.
May'll say there will not be a transition
Unless a final trade deal is agreed
By next summer, within less than a year.
A trade deal will take several years to reach
So there will not be a transition or
An exit fee, and there will be 'no deal'.
The UK'll want to grab a deal and run
As jackdaws snatch bread from a bird table
Or blue tits beak a nut and fly away,
But there'll be nothing to take, just silence
And cowslips waving on a windy bank.
So nothing will have changed, ahead's no deal,
Just a snake slithering off into long grass.
And all the time there is a ticking clock.
So turn your back on Europe, come with me.
Tell your leaders that the US will save
The UK's economy when it's left
The EU and has a whopping trade gap.
The UK's in a mess, it's on its knees.
The Government's not the faintest idea
Where it's all going. There'll be no progress.
She'll struggle to get her Brexit Bill through.
A final deal must also be approved
And ratified by the House of Commons,
And it's a minority Government
With too few MPs to win Commons votes.
Brussels is prepared for the fall of May.
It's going badly, you must come with me.

Minerva: King George the Third, you have something to say?

(GEORGE III *stands in the spotlight.*)

George III: First British Empire was American,

UK should unite with America.

Prince Charles: The UK will always have a special
Relationship with the US, but as
An important power in its own right.
It has the fifth-largest military
In the world, and its new aircraft-carrier
Has over four acres for forty planes.
The UK must stand on its own two feet.
It cannot be an American state.

(CHORUS OF ROYAL HOUSEHOLD STAFF, *loud
whispering.*)

Chorus of
royal house-
hold staff: Now it's about America. Oh dear,
What kind of UK is ahead of us?
UK, Europe, the US, it's all so
Unsettling, disturbing. What's our future?
We shudder at coming uncertainty.

(ASTRAEA, *goddess of fairness, stands in the spotlight.*)

Astraea: I'm Astraea, the goddess of fairness.
You must work for a just and fair UK
That spreads equality by borrowing.
The country should be separate from the world
So its wealth can be redistributed
And State ownership be revived once more,
So all can live at an equal standard –

(PENIA, *goddess of poverty, stands in the spotlight.*)

Penia: I'm Penia, the goddess of poverty.
Set an example, live like a pauper –

Minerva: Keir Hardie, the Labour Party's founder.

                    (KEIR HARDIE, *founder of the Labour Party and*
                    therefore of British socialism, stands in the spotlight. He
                    speaks with a Scottish accent.)

Keir Hardie: Socialism in one country, you should
                    Live at the level of those you will rule.

Prince Charles: As King of the UK I will accept
                    Whatever Government is elected.
                    But on State ownership I must point out
                    That there would have to be huge borrowing
                    To renationalise rail and energy
                    At a time when there is a deficit
                    And things are uncertain due to Brexit.
                    The borrowing will have to be repaid
                    And that will burden the British people.

Britannia: Your Royal Highness, their wealth tax will pay.
                    Labour's waiting for the Conservatives
                    To split over Brexit so they'll take power.
                    Labour wants a 20-per-cent wealth tax
                    On the top one per cent, which they believe
                    Will raise 800 billion pounds in one
                    Hit, a whole year's Government receipts. It
                    Need not be paid till death but interest at
                    Three per cent must be paid, and this will raise
                    Twenty-four billion pounds per annum. So
                    They can forgive all student loans, costing
                    Twelve billion pounds a year, and still put cash
                    Into the health service, rail, energy.
                    There will be huge international damage.
                    Inward investment will dry up, there will
                    Be a property market crisis. It
                    Will take ten years to get them out. Meanwhile

They will enrich themselves along the way
Like the Bolsheviks who they take after.

Keir Hardie: Socialism in one country requires
A wealth tax. This should be kept quiet until
The Socialists are ready to take power.

(PHEME, *goddess of rumour, stands in the spotlight.*)

Pheme: But hang on, you've all forgotten one thing.
I am Pheme, the goddess of rumour,
Report and gossip, sorry to push in.
I read your press for fame and good repute,
And infamy and scandal, and there's doubt
As to who should be the UK's next King.
Recent TV programmes on Diana –

Minerva: Pheme, enough. Enough, I say, enough
There are conflicting views on all that's passed.
The monarchy's hereditary, Prince Charles
Will be King of the UK, and all else
Is irrelevant rumour and gossip.
Eris, the goddess of strife and discord,
Of *chaos*, has no place in this debate.
The question is, the UK's destiny,
And what is in the next King's mind on this.

Prince Charles: My mind is filled with a cacophony
Of discordant voices and disorder,
Like parakeets squawking in an oak tree.
I see what the UK should not become
But am perplexed at what it should now be.

Minerva: We are all clear that the UK now has
A new destiny, but we all differ
On what that global destiny should be.

32

Listen to what the Kings and leaders say.

(CHORUS OF NINE SHADES OF KINGS AND LEADERS *stands in the spotlight*: ALFRED, HAROLD II, WILLIAM THE CONQUEROR, HENRY II, HENRY VIII, GEORGE III, PALMERSTON, CHURCHILL *and* KEIR HARDIE.)

Chorus of nine
Kings and
leaders: We, historical Kings and past leaders,
                All want the UK to succeed again.
                We see beyond limiting nation-states
                And see beyond their future global trade.
                Trade figures are important, but the task
                Is to look beyond the economy
                To a vibrant role the UK can find
                That solves its people's problems and the world's.
                Britannia and Europa, Columbia
                And Astraea, your advice is narrow,
                Insular, limiting to one nation
                Or region, and not open to the world.
                Minerva, come up with a new vision,
                An innovative dream that all can share.
                Minerva, bestow wisdom on this Prince.

(CHORUS OF ROYAL HOUSEHOLD STAFF, *loud whispering*.)

Chorus of
royal house-
hold staff: Poor Charles's mind is full of discordance,
                So are our minds. It's all so confusing.
                Where is Brexit leading? Nobody says.
                Let's hope 'Minerva' knows the way forward.

Masque

(MINERVA leads PRINCE CHARLES from the throne down the three red-carpeted steps and stands him on the red carpet so he can see both screens. Both are in the spotlight.)

Minerva: Your Royal Highness, the UN has failed.
               The UN dignitaries need new thinking.

               (On the right screen a CHORUS OF UN DIGNITARIES.)

Chorus of UN
dignitaries: We UN dignitaries are in despair.
               Alas, we are despondent at the world.
               We are in misery and wretchedness.
               We are unable to control nations.
               Right now, despite all our constant efforts
               And meetings of the General Assembly
               And Security Council, seventy-two
               Wars[3] are being fought on all continents
               And we have failed to prevent one hundred
               And sixty-two wars[4] since the Second World War.
               And despite our disarmament programs
               There are still fourteen thousand nine hundred
               Nuclear weapons terrorists must not seize
               From stores in remote places and let off
               A dirty bomb in a Western city.
               Alas, keeping the peace is really hard.
               It seems we're fighting a losing battle
               And disorder's winning, we're struggling.
               We need a new system to keep order.

Minerva: Your Royal Highness, look with sympathy

At the plight of the suffering of the world.

(*On the right screen a* CHORUS OF SUFFERING
PEOPLES *drawn from every continent.*)

Chorus of
suffering
peoples:

We are the suffering peoples of the world.
More than 1.3^5 billion live on less
Than one dollar twenty-five cents a day;
More than three billion, nearly half the world's
Population, on less than two dollars
Fifty cents a day. Eight hundred and five
Million do not have enough food to eat.
We go bare-footed, thin from starvation,
We squat in bombed houses, watch beheadings.
We are cowed and comply, and long for change.
We have no hope, we just endure each day.
Life for us is a Hell, we feel listless.
Who will deliver us from daily grind?
Who will give us a vision of new life
That liberates us from our drudgery?

Minerva:

The wretched of backward countries cry out.
You are going to be King of the fifth-
Largest economy and fifth-largest
Military power in the world, behind
The US, Russia, China, India,
Who are all too regionalised to help.
The top four all have national consciousness.
You are the fifth, and you are listening
And you can solve their problems, you can see
Beyond the nation-state to a World State.
A democratic World State was foreseen
By Presidents Truman and Eisenhower,
By Einstein, who was very wise, Churchill,

Russell, Gandhi and John F. Kennedy,
And Gorbachev; a respectable line,
Mentors you may be pleased to emulate.

Prince Charles: Though I've not thought that the UK should be
Under a World State, I've an open mind.
I see all nation-states as a great field
Of sunflowers that are turned towards the sun.

Minerva: I show you the future decades from now
As Zeus would like it to unfold so long
As human free will makes the right choices
For the future to resemble what you
Will now see in our virtual projection.

(*On the left screen delegates at the UN General Assembly.*
CHORUS OF ROYAL HOUSEHOLD STAFF, *loud whispering.*)

Chorus of
royal house-
hold staff: This is it, look, she's showing the future.
She's telling him what the UK can do
To be a global power in the future.
How will a new World State improve the lot
Of the suffering peoples of the world?
Let's hope it goes beyond wishful trade deals
That won't happen, let's hope it's realistic.

(*As her speech continues* MINERVA *shows other images
from her projection of the future on the left screen.*)

Minerva: See, the democratic World Government
Is in session in its World Parliament,
Using the UN General Assembly
Which it has superseded. Look closely.

There are 850 representatives[6]
From constituencies throughout the world.

(*On the left screen the scene moves to the World Senate.*)

Look again, the World Senate with ninety-
Two senators all elected world-wide.

Prince Charles: How will a nation-state – my own UK –
Differ from now under this new World State?

Minerva: All nation-states remain the same but see,
There is a federal, supranationalist
Level that includes the Senate, and look
As we fly over the current hot spots –
Syria, Afghanistan, other war zones –
For there is peace, war has been abolished.
See the peace-keeping force in those ruins
And look, those stores of nuclear weapons,
See those bombs are locked up in warehouses,
All nuclear bombs have been confiscated.
And look, as we fly over South Sudan,
Harvests, starvation's a thing of the past.
And look in all the earth's backward regions,
See, full employment, good health, no disease,
Hunger has gone, and poverty's no more.
All have enough, humankind is happy.
And look at the temperature, and those crops.
Global warming's coped with, the environment.
All done through viewing the world through the eyes
Of Universalism: a World State's
Political Universalism.
All these miraculous developments
Can be traced back to a political
Reorganisation by a federal
Body that has cured all the suffering

In the world, all you witnessed lamenting.
All humankind's in a Peaceful Era
And lives in an age of prosperity.

Prince Charles: I am amazed. And the UK has reaped
The same benefits and is prospering?

Minerva: Yes, it's beyond all considerations
Of its relationship with the EU,
It's beyond EU negotiations.
The UK's future's outside the EU,
It's regardless of a deal or 'no deal'.
It's linked to all states through this new World State,
The United Federation of the World.
And now I show you how the world got there
And all the suffering had their problems solved.
Look, that's you standing in the old UN
Out there in the not too distant future
And addressing from the raised podium
All the General Assembly's delegates,
In our mock-up, our virtual projection.
I know you're supposed to take your cue from
The British Government as you must be
A constitutional monarch, but you
Have championed causes as the Prince of Wales
To do with the environment, and you –
As it's in your nature – will continue
To champion causes when King, argue
Your case and win support. I know you will
Be a proactive King, not a yes-man.
I'm not surprised that you are standing there,
Standing up for what is right as usual
As you have always done, as your own man.
You've found your destiny, to link the world.
The UK's destiny is to promote
A new view of how humankind can live

At peace together in constituencies
Based on the nation-states but now at one,
Co-operative, not competitive,
And in harmony with the universe.
Look, you've brought in a Golden Age that seems
A Paradise to all who knew the past,
Its nightmare wars and nuclear weapons,
Famine and hunger, pollution, disease
And massive inequalities of wealth.
The UK is a global power that builds
A better world for all through its model.
And energy's for all. See, oligarchs
Can no longer make war for oil and gas
And drive oil and gas pipes through hostile lands.
From what you've seen, have you now found your
 role?

(PRINCE CHARLES *has had conflicting advice and is
in conflict. He soliloquises.*)

Prince Charles: My mind is simmering from all I've heard,
I have to make sense of these differing views.
The future destiny of the UK –
All that has been said on the subject by
Britannia, Europa, Columbia –
Seems so important, yet when it is seen
From the perspective of the universe,
Of the lives of the beasts, insects and birds,
It seems so insignificant.... My role.
I have to choose the wisest course, it's hard.
So what does it mean to be truly wise?

Minerva: Wisdom's better recognised than defined,
As is folly, it's opposite. All know
A fool when they see one and hear him speak.
I know if someone who holds forth is wise.

What's said shows sound judgement and
    discernment.
Wise men judge soundly and are discerning,
And can perceive the best path to their goal,
Have sound judgement in choosing means and ends
And common sense in practical affairs.
But in contrast, a 'fool' is like 'bellows' –
The Latin *follis* means 'a leather bag',
'A pair of bellows' and so 'a wind-bag' –
And is deficient in judgement and sense,
And is weak-minded, idiotic wind.
Folly is foolishness, lack of good sense.
There's a dialectic of opposites:
Humans can learn what it means to be wise
By being aware of what folly is
And recognising the path they must take.
Wisdom always discerns the direction
That pioneers a country's better way.
Folly claims to know the destination,
Its confidence leads citizens astray.
The highest Wisdom flows into the mind's
Higher consciousness from the beyond, from
The Light, Supreme Thought in the universe.
Wisdom flows into *me* from Supreme Thought,
It streams into my head as shafts of Light.
The best way to be wise is to open
To the mysterious Light religions know,
The Light of Zeus which will surround your head
Like a halo that's full of inner power
When you are crowned at your coronation
And implement the divine right of kings.
Since your mother was crowned, the UK's changed.
It's now a godless, foolish nation-state,
Sees Christmas and Easter as fairy tales.
A wise man is aware of the divine
As you are aware of the many faiths.

By your example on your red-gold throne
You can lead your sick Kingdom back to health.
O look, Apollo's here, to tell you more.

(APOLLO, *god of Light and the sun, appears on the left screen.*)

Apollo: I, Apollo, must come in at this point.
I am god of the Light, called the sun-god
As a symbol so all can understand –
I've never pushed the sun across the sky
Like a beetle pushing a ball of dung;
Also god of poetry and oracles.
Do not forget that all of humankind
Have souls that can equally see the Light –
Have equal potentiality to see
It when they choose to open to its power
Behind their rational, social, blocking 'I' –
And so are equal in terms of the Light
Though all are diverse and all are different.
Whoever founds the global World State should
Found it on the Light, which makes all equal.

Minerva: Wisely spoken, Apollo. Your Highness,
Can you now see the UK's destiny
And can you see yourself bringing it in?

(CHORUS OF ROYAL HOUSEHOLD STAFF, *loud whispering.*)

Chorus of
royal house-
hold staff: What will he say? Will we now see what kind
Of King he'll be? What is the UK's role
When it leaves the EU? Do we now know?
What's going on? What are they doing here?

Prince Charles: Yes. I will have several roles and voices
Like an actor who puts on different masks,
And will operate at several levels.
First and foremost I'll be the UK's King
And do my duty at national level
And not engage in party politics.
But then my family are European,
With roots in Germany. When there's a deal,
Though the UK will have left the EU
I will stay closely involved with Europe
And my role at the regional level.
We have to accept the vote for Brexit
But we can be as we were forty-five
Years ago, back in 1972
Before we joined Europe's Common Market.
And I must stay close to America
At the separate transatlantic level
And make sure we continue our special
Relationship, but the UK will not
Become America's fifty-first state.
But above all I'll have a global role.
Through royal tours and video conferences
I will stay in touch with our imperial lands
And nurture links within the Commonwealth,
At a historical global level.
More than that, just as the UK will trade
With all the world's nations and I will meet
All world leaders to cement our trade links,
Maintain and enhance British influence,
Promote British values and business goals
And advance British foreign policy,
I will take on an additional role,
To discuss the future with world leaders
At a federal, supranational level.
With the permission of our Government
I must work to benefit humankind

For all are spiritually equal
Before the Light that permeates our lives,
Which I will contemplate within my soul.
I must be as still as a butterfly
Settled on lilac buddleia in bloom,
As still as a yellow water lily
That smiles like the sun in a muddy pond
And is oblivious of croaking frogs
And dragonflies that hover in mid-air.
As King of the UK, I'll be the Head
Of the Church of England, but will also
Rule over subjects who have other faiths.
There are several faiths but all faiths are one.
There are several paths up a high mountain
But at its summit all see the same sun.
I must work for fairness in the UK
But also for Universalism,
For I must not ignore all humankind.
If an opportunity's presented,
Having consulted with our Government,
And free to offer thoughts and suggestions,
I must, with tactful diplomacy, talk
Political Universalism
To all world leaders through their delegates
At the UN's General Assembly,
For the true context of UK-EU
Negotiations is the towering
Prospect that there will be a new World State
That enfolds all nation-states and regions
As starry night sky blankets humankind.
I must make it clear that the UK's role
Includes improving world security
Which means making the UN effective
And that this is best done by the UK's
Diplomatic, indeed visionary
Initiative and innovatory plan

For a partly-federal World Government
That leaves all nation-states in power at home
But restricts power abroad to bring in peace.
As King of the UK I'll have no view
On this, but the merits of peace speak for
Themselves and are greatly to be desired.
Global Britain will be a world power, yes,
But may, during the coming months and years
Come to seek support for a federal world
To control world peace and disarmament,
Famine, disease and the environment,
And tackle poverty through world finance
The dream's to create a democratic,
Elected World State that can impose peace.
I hope, if I can intrigue it in time,
My reign will call for a new world vision.
That will be another mask I will wear.
I will reign from my nation-state but will
Inspire a new deal for humanity.
Let it be known, the Carolingian Age
Will seek to bring a universal peace
To humankind, regardless of nation.

(*The* SHADES OF NINE KINGS AND LEADERS
and goddesses enthusiastically applaud. MINERVA
*indicates that he should return up the three steps and sit
on the throne. She follows him. She now holds a golden
crown, standing in the spotlight.*)

Minerva: Your Royal Highness, you have synthesised
All the views you've heard, you have accepted
The humanitarian concerns behind
My vision, and we all can see that you
Will be a King with higher consciousness
And a clear mind who'll speak for humankind.
You can now see the correct way ahead.

And so I bestow my Wisdom on you
Through this symbolic crown, and I crown you
'King Charles the Wise' who found his global role:
To restore peace and order to the world.

(*All the* SHADES OF NINE KINGS AND LEADERS
*and the goddesses echo "King Charles the Wise" and
enthusiastically applaud.*)

Prince Charles
(aside):   The French king Charles the Fifth was 'Charles the
                Wise'.
            He reconquered territories in France
            Ceded in 1360 to England.

(CHORUS OF ROYAL HOUSEHOLD STAFF, *loud
whispering.*)

Chorus of
royal house-
hold staff: He's been 'crowned' on the throne 'King Charles
                the Wise'.
            They must be making a video, but where
            Is their camera? It looks as if it's real.
            She called him 'Charles the Wise'. It's all so strange.
            What's happening? What does it mean for us?
            Is global Britain a reality?
            Can we be optimistic once again?

Revels

(*Immediately afterwards.* PRINCE CHARLES *is still sitting on the throne. There is rejoicing from those in the Throne Room. On the left screen there is a close-up still of* MINERVA *crowning the* PRINCE OF WALES, *to joyful music. There is celebratory dancing among the* SHADES OF NINE KINGS AND LEADERS *and goddesses. This stops abruptly when on the right screen appears a* CHORUS OF EIGHT DISTINGUISHED SUPPORTERS *of a new World State:* TRUMAN, EISENHOWER, EINSTEIN, CHURCHILL, RUSSELL, GANDHI, J.F. KENNEDY *and* GORBACHEV.)

Chorus of eight
distinguished
supporters:

We eight supporters of a new World State
Welcome you to our ranks and applaud you.
We were shocked by the first atomic bomb
And sought a safer world system that would
Control all weapons of mass destruction,
Prevent all wars in which they might be used.
We want a responsible world order
That can abolish war and improve lives,
And the United Nations is not this.
We long for a World State that can create
A better world for wretched humankind
And we will be pleased if you support this.

(*As their faces fade from the screen* MINERVA *speaks.*)

Minerva:

Thank you, distinguished, celebrated friends.
But now I see Britannia wants to speak.

Britannia: I'm sorry to interrupt your revels.
I have reservations on all we've heard.
Global Britain's Britain dominating
The world as its fifth-most-powerful nation,
Not being under a conglomerate,
Subordinate to world federalism.

Prince Charles: But global Britain will be a big power.
It will soon have two aircraft-carriers:
HMS *Queen Elizabeth*, now in
Portsmouth, with its motto '*Semper eadem*',
'Always the same', stressing the dominance
Of the fleets of Richard the Lionheart,
Henry the Eighth and Admiral Nelson;
And HMS *Prince of Wales*, named to me,
Which is nearly finished. And with their planes
They'll put the UK among the foremost
Nation-states in the world, and therefore one
Of the main diplomatic countries that
Can renegotiate the world order
And strengthen the role of the UN by
Replacing it with legally-based power
To abolish all war and nuclear bombs.
I will be a constitutional monarch
But I'll be my own man and just because
The Queen is not known for initiatives
I do not have to be docile, passive,
I can have opinions and share them – as
A grasshopper saws in the summer grass –
With the Prime Minister at our meetings.
Who is to say I cannot try to shape
British policy when my PM comes?
And just as I make royal tours abroad
And promote the UK to foreign powers
As a perfect, sweet-smelling, satin rose,
And present the UK in a good light

To foreign leaders in our discussions,
Who's to say I can't mention the merits
Of a new international structure
That can outlaw war and nuclear weapons,
And solve the world's problems, the air attacks
That cause the refugees, terrorism
And dreadful beheadings, the starvation
And treatable disease that blight the poor?
The new idea the UK can advance
Is a mini-world-federalism.
The federal bit solves all the world's problems
The UN can't solve as it lacks true power.
As King I will be very persuasive,
As King of global Britain I will call
For help for the downtrodden and the three
Billion world citizens who live on less
Than 2.5^7 measly dollars a day.
I am a human being before a King.
I'll be a spokesman for humanity.
We all share the beauty of our planet:
White cherry blossom that resembles snow.

(CHORUS OF ROYAL HOUSEHOLD STAFF, *loud
whispering.*)

Chorus of
royal house-
hold staff: He's going to do it, he's looking beyond
These shores to the whole world, he is going
To be King of both here and everywhere.
He's going to be a universal King.
We don't understand, must be a video.

Minerva: And you will oversee Britain's progress
From early Kings and pastoral origins
To global sway like a river that glides

From narrow source to a wide estuary
And merges with the boundless ocean that
Surrounds the globe and all its continents.
You will culminate a long, slow movement.
Clio, the Muse of history, can tell how.

(CLIO *speaks. The men she names stand in the spotlight when their names are called.*)

Clio: Long ago Alfred united England
And Alfred the occupying Danes, and then
Harold's Saxons fought off the Norwegians
But fell to Duke William and his Normans
Who conquered and held the whole of England.
Then Henry the Second ruled swathes of France
And Henry the Eighth defended England
And united with Wales and formed Britain.
Then James the Sixth of Scotland became King
And Queen Anne's England's union with Scotland
Enlarged Britain, which became Great Britain.
Then George the Third's American Empire
Swelled British power across the Atlantic
And Union with Ireland bore the UK.
Then Palmerston advanced UK interests
And paved the way for the Second Empire.
And Churchill led the UK when it ruled
A quarter of the world, although the war
Led to loss of empire, and oversaw
Decolonising into Commonwealth.
For forty-five years the UK has been
Within the EU but is returning
To how it was in 1972,
Independent and in control once more,
And will continue its Commonwealth flow
And reconnect with its great-power vision
That will make it seem to have been asleep

During its membership of the EU.
A great nation-state is awakening –
As if the slumbering giant in seven-league boots
Of European magical folklore
Whose stride is twenty miles, were sitting up –
And will astound the world with its great deeds,
And the greatest, certainly the noblest,
Will be to redraw the global structure
Through its innovative thinking, which you,
In your general discussions as they rise,
Will be able to advance to leaders.
But a warning. The UK may break up,
It's in danger of splitting into four,
Declining from a united kingdom
Into a federation of nations
In a looser, more separate structure
With England having its own new devolved
Parliament, while Europe may soon expand –
Now it can have its own army without
Opposition from the UK, which wants
Its own army to persist as a power –
Into a United States of Europe.

Minerva: So you now have a vision of order,
And see that the future is globalised,
That isolationism is folly.
And now I show you a future image.

(PRINCE CHARLES *leaves the throne, still wearing*
Minerva's crown, and returns down the three steps to
where he can see the screens. He stands in the spotlight.
On the left screen, PRINCE CHARLES *sits on a throne*
in Westminster Abbey. A still of this image remains on
the left screen until the end of the masque.)

That's you at your coronation, cheered on

By rejoicings of revellers all round
The world, who are uplifted and inspired
By your conviction, pursuit of what's right.

(PRINCE CHARLES *is silent*.)

Look, the suffering peoples salute you.

(*On the right screen, the* CHORUS OF SUFFERING
PEOPLES.)

Chorus of
suffering
peoples:

How long we've waited for deliverance.
We sit in shade and chew our cheeks for food.
We sleep in rubble like wild animals.
We lie in torpor in dusty sunsets.
Our lifetimes have slipped by and no one's helped.
But now, after all these years, there is hope.
Each nation-state can be grouped together,
Powerful people may sort out our problems.
We are so grateful that we're remembered.
We want to live normal lives like most folk.
We don't want to cross sea on leaky rafts.
Please help us quickly, we can't take much more.
Thank you for giving us a bright future.
Your Majesty, please speak for us, please help.
We honour you as you sit on your throne,
And welcome a new Carolingian Age
When you defend all people from all faiths
As King in a Universalist world.
Please lead us into improving our lives.

(CHORUS OF ROYAL HOUSEHOLD STAFF, *loud whispering*.)

Chorus of royal household staff:	It must be a film. Look, he has been crowned In Westminster Abbey. The Queen's not dead. He must be acting a future event For a film. We are really confused now. The future's a nightmare, it makes no sense.
Minerva:	Our past Kings and leaders want to come in.

(*The* CHORUS OF NINE KINGS AND LEADERS *stands in the spotlight.*)

Chorus of nine Kings and leaders:	We historical Kings and past leaders Are overjoyed that you will now support A global Britain with a Commonwealth That can do trade deals and be a beacon For global free trade, and slowly replace The EU's single market, a large *bloc* Of nation-states' peoples who speak English; And that will request world leaders to call For a Constitutional Convention In the UN to set up a World State With elected representatives and A federal tier that can declare all war Illegal and impound all nuclear bombs And deliver a Golden Age of Peace To desperate humankind for a long while.
Minerva:	And our goddesses have something to say.

(A CHORUS OF THE FIVE GODDESSES *stands in the spotlight:* BRITANNIA, EUROPA, COLUMBIA, ASTRAEA *and* PHEME.)

Chorus of five goddesses:	We goddesses have our own perspectives
	And speak for areas we specialise in
	And are responsible for to great Zeus.
	But beyond our narrow briefs we all look
	For what will benefit all humankind,
	And we are delighted that there's a plan
	To create a world order that's untried
	And bring in a World State with fresh thinking
	That all can take part in, so all belong.
	We all encourage you in your contacts
	And hope you'll help get a supranational
	Movement under way that will result in
	A new world structure that benefits all.

Minerva:	Look, these well-known historical leaders
	From the British Empire and Commonwealth
	Want to address you on global Britain.

(*On the right screen appears a* CHORUS OF HISTORICAL LEADERS FROM THE BRITISH EMPIRE AND COMMONWEALTH, *all now dead.* GANDHI, NEHRU *and* NKRUMAH *can be seen. The still from* KING CHARLES's *coronation is still up on the left screen.*)

Chorus of leaders from British Empire and Commonwealth:	We leaders from the past British Empire
	And early Commonwealth, all dominions,
	Greet you from every continent, many
	From Africa and India, all nations
	Where there was once British imperial rule.
	We rejoice that the UK will return

To its old role of linking with the world
As it did before it entered Europe.
All our countries are crying out for peace,
The end of terrorism, enough food,
And trading with the UK will be good,
And joining a World State while retaining
Internal independence will suit them.
We welcome a new structure for the world.
We look forward to benefiting from
New thinking and new order in the world.

Minerva: Look, the British people are crowding in.

(*On the right screen, the* CHORUS OF BRITISH
PEOPLE, *all classes and professions, some still in suits
and some still casually dressed.*)

Chorus of
British people: We, the British people, welcome a time
When we can all be better off from trade
With all the countries in the world and be
A global power once more in our own right,
Make our own decisions on war and peace.
Once more we will be valued round the world.
Again we will be innovative as
We invented the steam engine, TV,
The internet, and there is more to come.
We are a nation-state that gives to all
And we will pioneer a new World State.
British ingenuity will remake
The world for our schoolchildren and their heirs.
We will still influence the world's progress.
We're optimistic about the future
And hope you'll implement what we have dreamed.

Minerva: And now see the world's united peoples.

(*On the right screen, a* CHORUS OF THE WORLD'S UNITED PEOPLES *in the future. Men, women and children of every nationality and colour.*)

Chorus of the
world's united
peoples:

We, the world's united peoples, welcome
Global Britain, which made a huge difference.
Now thanks to the British initiative
We are all living in one federal state
With full employment and prosperity.
In each region there's universal peace.
We all have stable families and homes
And under central planning there's enough
For everybody as we go about
Our business and leisure with our loved ones.
We celebrate the UK which saw this
And made sure the world implemented peace.

Minerva:

The nine Muses send you a rare tribute.

(*On the right screen, a* CHORUS OF THE NINE MUSES.)

Chorus of nine
Muses:

We, the Nine Muses, hail our turning-point.
In the last century the arts lost their way
Amid the wars of nation-states, world wars
And numerous conflicts that blocked inner flow.
Doodle poems, squiggle paintings and shrieked
Music expressed the ego, not the soul.
Poor literature was praised, good derided.
But now under the supranational
World State the arts are in a Golden Age.
Profound works flourish. Shallow work is seen
For what it is, and in our stable time

The soul has the tranquillity to delve
And see beyond daily life to the One.
Our artists convey a sense of purpose
And deep understanding of the universe.
Poets like dressmakers sew sequins on
Their dress-like works: images of all life.
Your reign was a turning-point, we hail you
And the vision of unity brought in
By Universalist Carolingians.

Minerva: Who are these intruders in our revels?

(*On the right screen, a* CHORUS OF FIVE WORLD
LEADERS: TRUMP, PUTIN, XI-JINPING, JUNCKER
and SINGH, *the leaders of the US, the Russian
Federation, China, the European Union and India.*)

Chorus of five
world leaders: We leaders of America, Russia,
China, Europe and India are lost.
We want to stop migrants and terrorists,
Wars, famine and disease but can't see how.
The UN is not strong enough, it just
Listens to nation-states that disagree.
We don't know how to improve world order.
No one listens to threats, we all want peace.
Will someone please explain what we should do.

(MINERVA *addresses* PRINCE CHARLES.)

Minerva: We're back in the present, the future's gone.
Our virtual projection is now over.
The world is crying out for new order.
You will champion causes as your own man.
You will offer leadership that's missing.
And we all hope you'll work for a World State.

(The still of KING CHARLES's *coronation is still on the left screen.)*

Prince Charles: I am deeply humbled by all I've seen.
I'm grateful to all those who've greeted me
From the present and, of course, the future
As joyful swallows from a distant shore
Swoop and skim to and fro in a meadow.
I will try to be worthy of them all.
As King I will act out my global role
Regardless of EU deal or 'no deal'
Or even if there's no Brexit at all.
When I meet world leaders I will discuss
The misery of war and if it can
Be resolved by working to introduce
A new world structure that benefits all
And resolves all environment issues.
I will keep humankind always in mind.
I will be a spokesman for all the poor
With a clear song like a blackbird's piping
In my looming Carolingian Age
And will proclaim it Universalist
And try to turn our miserable world
Into a Paradise for humankind.

(PRINCE CHARLES *takes his place back on the throne. The red box awaits him.*)

Minerva: Our revels now are ended. All on screen
Have melted into air as if spirits.
But now in 'Operation Hand-over'
You know what you are looking for, your role
In the UK's eventual destiny
When an innovative initiative
Can call for a new structure in the world
And for implementing the new World State

That Zeus and all the gods and goddesses
Hope the UK will manage to guide in.
I know you'll help for you are 'Charles the Wise'.
I have to return to great Zeus, so now
I bid you farewell till I come again,
And take my leave. You're Olympus's hope.

(MINERVA *walks out of the spotlight and disappears into the shadows, leaving* PRINCE CHARLES *alone, wearing* MINERVA's *golden crown. He resumes work on the Queen's red box.*)

Prince Charles: Perhaps all I've just seen has been a dream.
Perhaps thoughts materialised from my mind.
Perhaps I've been alone with this red box
And the people have been a waking dream
Projected from my imagination.

(*He raises his right hand to his head and removes* MINERVA's *crown. He muses.*)

But now I know the UK's destiny
And what my role as King will now involve.

(*He reads a paper from the red box.*)

Before I did not understand the words,
What the Government's position should be.
I could not see it, like a bat hanging
In a dark corner of a half-lit loft.
But now I know what I want it to be
And I can effortlessly see what's wrong,
What is not in this position paper,
And what it should say out of clarity.
I will make Brexit work and will stand for
The humanitarian approach to wars

That can become law under a World State.
I am resolved, I will be my own man
And, in alliance with Mount Olympus,
Which has crowned me with Wisdom I must use,
Will act out divine will to humankind
And leave the world a much, much better place.

(CHORUS OF ROYAL HOUSEHOLD STAFF, *loud whispering*.)

Chorus of royal household staff:	They all believe something good has happened. They're speaking as if they're in the future. Whatever's going on, it's turned out well. He's going to make the post-Brexit world work. He'll have a good future when he is King And he will change things for all humankind.
Page:	I am waiting to carry his red box Back to the Office of the Prince of Wales.
Maid:	I'll clear away the tea tray when he leaves.
Footman:	I'll click off the spotlight when he retires.

Epilogue

(Mount Olympus. MINERVA *stands before* ZEUS, *who is seated on the Olympian throne. Both are spotlit.)*

Minerva:

Lord of all, you asked me to become your
Ambassador, visit the Prince of Wales
And guide him on the role of the UK,
After Brexit so he could be aware
Of your global plan for a new World State.
This I have done, and he will work with you,
He shares the humanitarian concerns
Behind your vision of an improved world.
Of course, he'll have to be first and foremost
King of the UK, a constitutional
Monarch who has to operate within
Strict guidelines given him by his Government,
But he will be defender of all faiths
And he cares about all humanity,
And in the course of his royal duties
In the UK's new role after Brexit,
If other leaders bring the subject up
He'll discuss the plight of all humankind
And the humanitarian issues
Whose solution is in new world structures
That will abolish war and strengthen peace.
He has a strong belief, as we'd all wish,
In a wise world Universalism,
He knows how strong global Britain can be,
And is aware that humanitarian
Concerns can be resolved by devising
New supranationalist world structures.
So now you've got someone who'll work with you,
Who'll be true to his UK and Europe
But also to the world, to humankind,

When he inherits the great British throne
And has his coronation. We've all seen
That what he says is very impressive,
And he'll soon be known as 'King Charles the Wise'.

Zeus: Thank you, my dearest goddess Minerva.
You've done excellently, just as I wished.
We are all fortunate that you can take
Your wisdom to the world, where foolish man
Has turned against true vision and pursues
His selfish interests and his nation-state's,
And make it stick. I congratulate you.
What are we to do when the President
Of the US rants and raves, sacks his staff,
And North Korea's leader threatens him
And both shout they will fire nuclear missiles?
It's like two children in a nursery
Playing with toy missiles in Lego walls.
Humankind deserves better leaders than
It has at present, we have to stop them
From acting out their own stupidity.
I will send you to the UN building
Next, to seek out the Secretary-General
Of the United Nations and persuade
Him to consider the merits of change,
Of moving to a federal world order
That can confiscate all nuclear missiles.
If he is receptive to a World State
With a World Government that can ban war,
Then he will empathise with visitors
Like the Prince of Wales and other leaders
And state the case for a Constitutional
Convention that can transform the UN.
I have thought that humankind can progress
To a World State sedately, when ready,
Without undue haste, but the behaviour

Of present world leaders makes it urgent.
We can't wait while blundering leaders make
Things worse with economic nationalism,
Protectionism, borders and high walls,
Populism, pro-nation-state-ism,
Self-first isolationism that goes
Against the direction of a World State.
We have to bring the World State forward or
There'll be no humankind to set it up.
I'm too old to put up with blundering
Any more. I'm fed up with dim half-wits,
With stubborn, disobedient leaders
Who mule-like won't budge from wrong points of
     view
And give democracy such a bad name.
I can still see ahead a Golden Age.
I hold fast to that vision the world needs:
An age of peace and of prosperity.
We can't wait any longer, we must push
For it before confused humanity
Devastates the earth with its crass mistakes,
Blights the planet with a nuclear winter.
We're bringing on the World State now, we need
More leaders like Prince Charles. And so I say,
Bravo Minerva and King Charles the Wise.
Onward to a peaceful and settled world
And the triumph of universal peace.

14–21 August; 22–24 September; 11–31 October;
1, 5, 8–9, 11–17 November; 9, 18 December 2017

Timeline

List of dates of key events referred to in *King Charles the Wise*

22 January 1963	Treaty of Friendship between France and West Germany signed by President de Gaulle and Chancellor Adenauer
23 June 2016	UK Referendum, UK votes to leave the European Union
28 March 2017	Prime Minister May signs a letter triggering Article 50
22 September 2017	Prime Minister May's speech in Florence
26 September 2017	Meeting between Donald Tusk, President of the European Council, and Prime Minister May
19–20 October 2017	European summit, held in the buildings of the Council of the European Union
29 March 2019	UK set to leave the European Union

Notes

1. 490, pronounced 'four hundred and ninety'.
2. 469, pronounced 'four six nine'.
3. For a list of the 72 wars, see Nicholas Hagger, *World State*, pp.268–281.
4. For a list of the 162 wars, see Nicholas Hagger, *World State*, pp.288–293.
5. 1.3, pronounced 'one point three'.
6. 850, pronounced 'eight fifty'.
7. 2.5, pronounced 'two point five'.

BOOKS

O-BOOKS

O is a symbol of the world, of oneness and unity; this eye represents knowledge and insight.